U.S. Department
of Transportation

**United States
Coast Guard**

Commandant (G-MVP)
United States Coast Guard

MAILING ADDRESS:
Washington, DC 20593-0001
Phone: (202) 267-2705

COMDTPUB P16721.31

2 NOV 1989

COMMANDANT PUBLICATION P16721.31

Subj: Merchant Marine Deck Examination Reference Book, STABILITY DATA REFERENCE BOOK.

1. PURPOSE. This publication contains reference material that may be needed by an applicant during an examination for a merchant marine deck license.

2. DISCUSSION.

   a. Applicants for merchant marine deck licenses taking an examination to determine their professional qualifications may be required to answer examination questions which are based on the material in this publication.

   b. The Coast Guard has converted to a computerized random generation system for creating examination modules. To streamline the process of creating module test booklets, where possible, the reference material needed to answer exam questions has been incorporated in Deck Examinations Reference Books. This allows applicants to view both the exam question and the reference material at the same time.

   c. Copies of this publication will be provided by the Regional Examination Centers (RECs) when applicants take an examination. This publication is available to the general public but only copies provided by the RECs may be used when completing an examination.

   d. The August 1989 edition of this publication contains all material required by questions in the question bank as of August 1989.

DISTRIBUTION - SDL No. 128

	a	b	c	d	e	f	g	h	i	j	k	l	m	n	o	p	q	r	s	t	u	v	w	x	y	z
A																										
B		1	1		1		1	1		1		1		1		1										
C				*									*													
D																										
E																										
F																										
G																										
H																										

* NON-STANDARD DISTRIBUTION:

INSTRUCTIONS

1. Some of the questions in the deck examination booklets require the use of trim and stability reference material to answer the question. All of the material necessary to these questions is contained in the appropriate Merchant Marine Deck Examination Reference Book.

2. If a question requires the use of trim / stability reference materials, it will be specifically stated in the stem of the question. For example, if the question in your examination booklet is, "The sailing drafts are: FWD 24'-03", AFT 25'-03" and the GM is 5.5 feet. Use the information in Section 1, the blue pages of the Stability Data Reference Book, to determine the available righting arm at 30 degrees inclination.", you must use Section 1 (the blue pages) of The Merchant Marine Deck Examination Reference Book, STABILITY DATA REFERENCE BOOK to answer the question.

3. The Merchant Marine Deck Examination Reference Book, STABILITY DATA REFERENCE BOOK, has three (3) sections. Each section has its own index and is color coded as follows:

1. Selected Stability Curves......................Blue Pages
2. Trim and Stability Book - S.S.American Mariner...White Pages
3. Trim and Stability Book - S.S.Northland.........Salmon Pages

4. Applicants taking an examination who wish to make a comment or protest concerning any material in this publication should complete a Comment/Protest form for the question involved and give it to the examiner.

5. Individuals not taking an examination who wish to make a comment on any material in this publication should send a written comment, citing this publication and the appropriate page, and paragraph or illustration commented on, to:

        Commandant (G-MVP-5)
        U.S. Coast Guard
        STABILITY DATA REFERENCE BOOK
        2100 Second Street SW
        Washington, DC 20593-0001

All written comments submitted by the general public will be reviewed prior to revising this publication. A heavy workload precludes the Merchant Marine Examination Branch from discussing comments over the telephone or responding to written comments. Your comments are welcomed and you will receive a letter or postcard indicating your comments were received.

TABLE OF CONTENTS

SECTION	PAGES
Selected Stability Curves	Blue Pages
Deadweight Scale	1
Hydrostatic Curves	2
Cross-Curves	3
*Statical Stability Curves	4
*Floodable Length Curve	5
Trim and Stability Book - S.S. AMERICAN MARINER	White Pages
Table of Principal Characteristics	Sheet 1
Trim Correction Table	Sheet 2
Hydrostatic Properties	Sheet 3
Free Surface Correction and Tank Cap.	Sheet 4
Gain in GM Table	Sheet 5
Required GM Curve	Sheet 6
*Loading Table	Sheet 7
*Loading Summary	Sheet 7A
Double Bottom Tankage	Sheet 8
Loading, Trim, and Stability Book - S.S. NORTHLAND	Salmon Pages
Table of Contents	Sheet i
Notes to Master	Sheet 1
Instructions - Trim and Stability	Sheet 2
Instructions - Hog and Sag	Sheet 3
Tank Capy. and CG	Sheet 4
Vertical Moments of Free Surface	Sheet 5
Trim Correction Table	Sheet 6
Curves of Form	Sheet 7
*Loading Summary	Sheet 81A
*Detail of Deadweight	Sheet 81B-C-D
*Longitudinal Bending Stresses	Sheet 81E

*Working copies of these pages are available to the candidate.

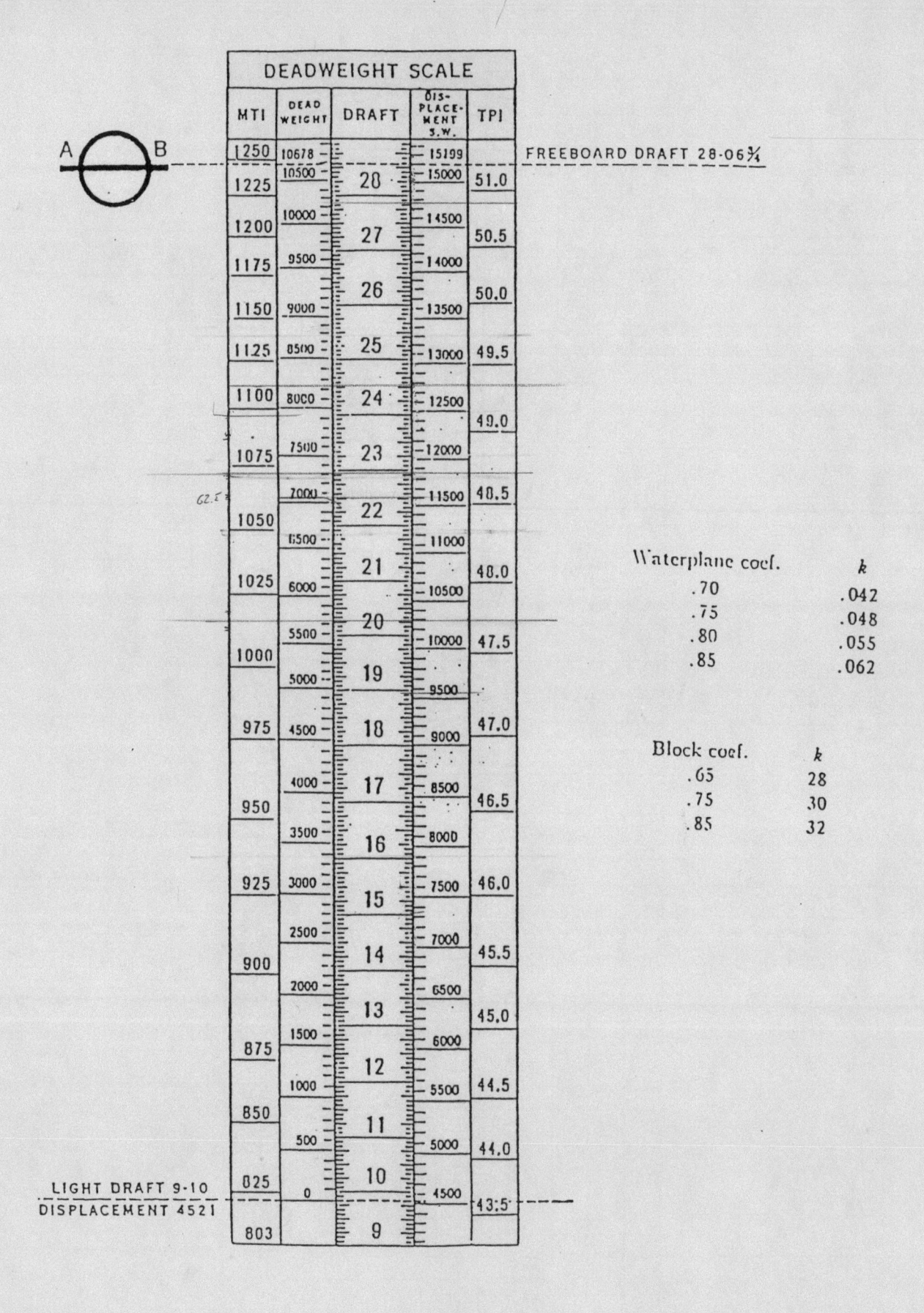

DEADWEIGHT SCALE

MTI	DEAD WEIGHT	DRAFT	DIS-PLACE-MENT S.W.	TPI
1250	10678		15199	
1225	10500	28	15000	51.0
1200	10000	27	14500	50.5
1175	9500		14000	
1150	9000	26	13500	50.0
1125	8500	25	13000	49.5
1100	8000	24	12500	
1075	7500	23	12000	49.0
1050	7000	22	11500	48.5
1025	6500	21	11000	48.0
	6000	20	10500	
1000	5500	19	10000	47.5
	5000		9500	
975	4500	18	9000	47.0
950	4000	17	8500	46.5
	3500	16	8000	
925	3000	15	7500	46.0
900	2500	14	7000	45.5
	2000	13	6500	45.0
875	1500		6000	
850	1000	12	5500	44.5
	500	11	5000	44.0
825	0	10	4500	43.5
803		9		

FREEBOARD DRAFT 28-06¾

LIGHT DRAFT 9-10
DISPLACEMENT 4521

Waterplane coef.	k
.70	.042
.75	.048
.80	.055
.85	.062

Block coef.	k
.65	28
.75	30
.85	32

HYDROSTATIC CURVES

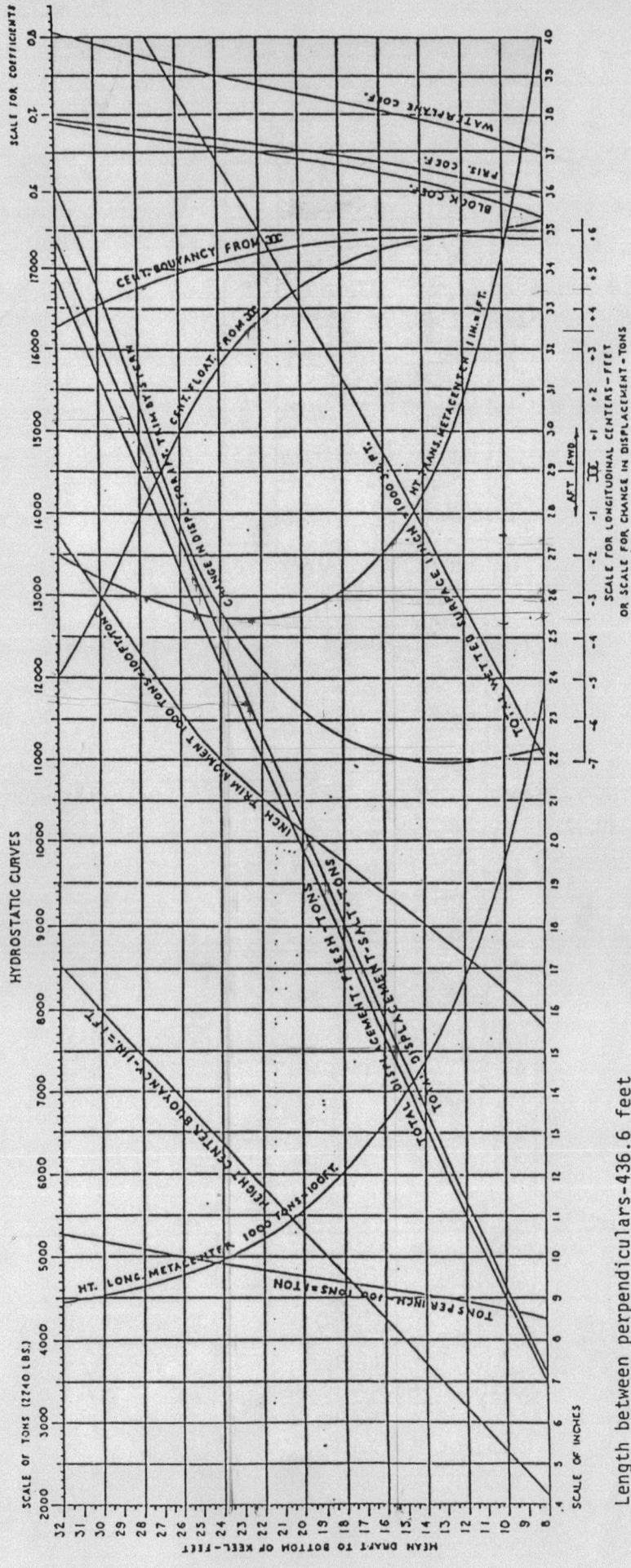

Length between perpendiculars—436.6 feet

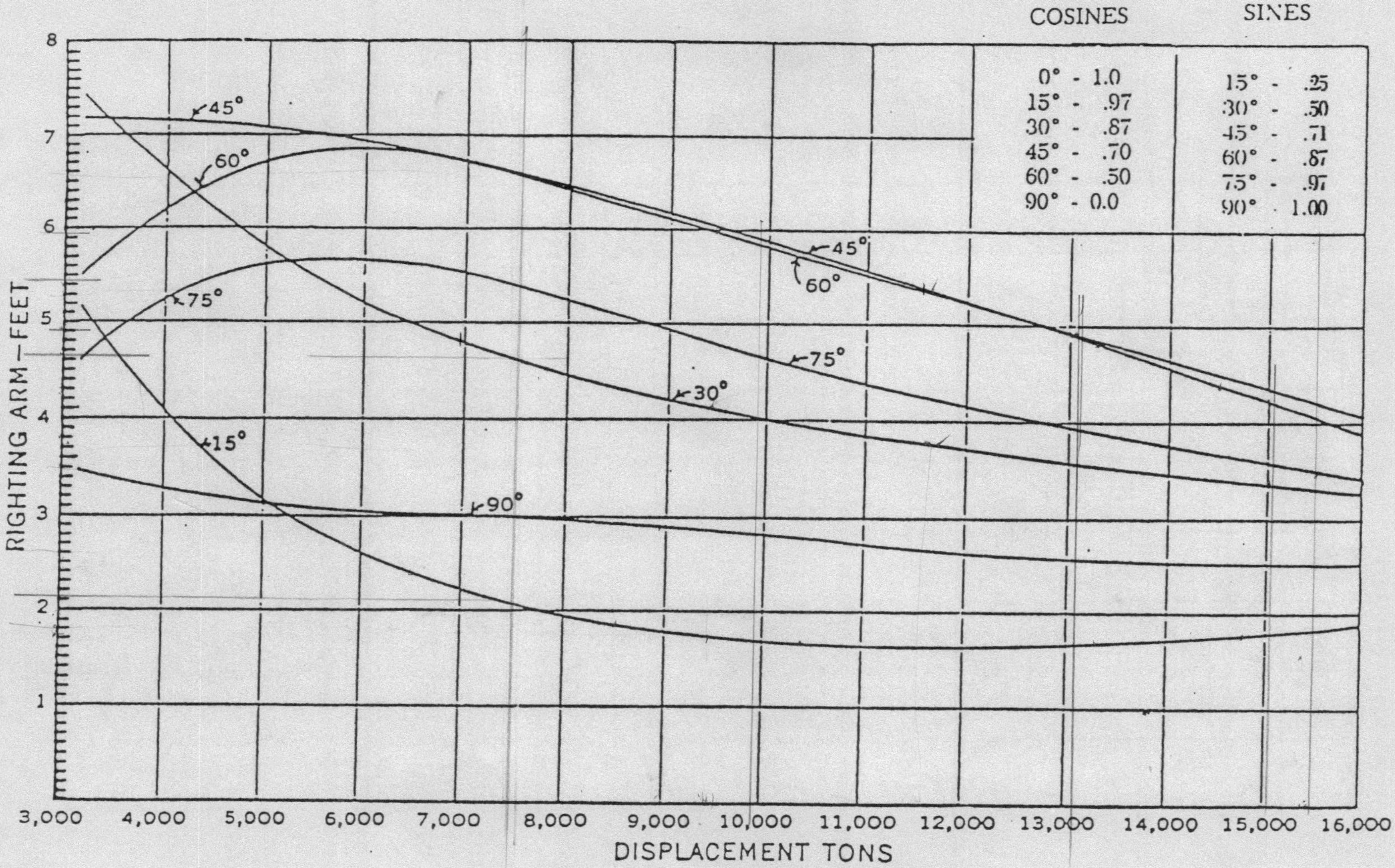

KG assumed to be 20.00 feet

Statical stability curves.

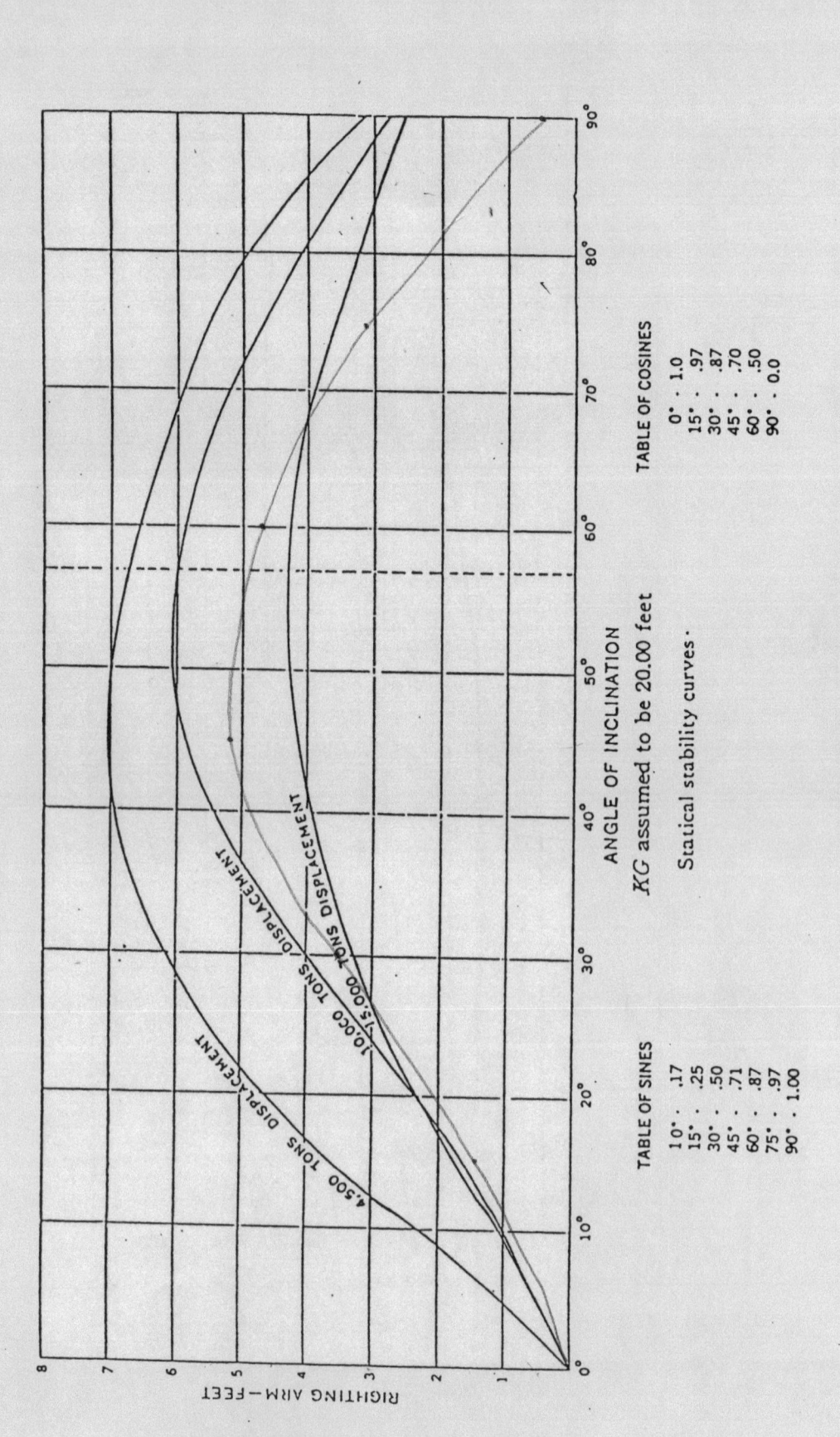

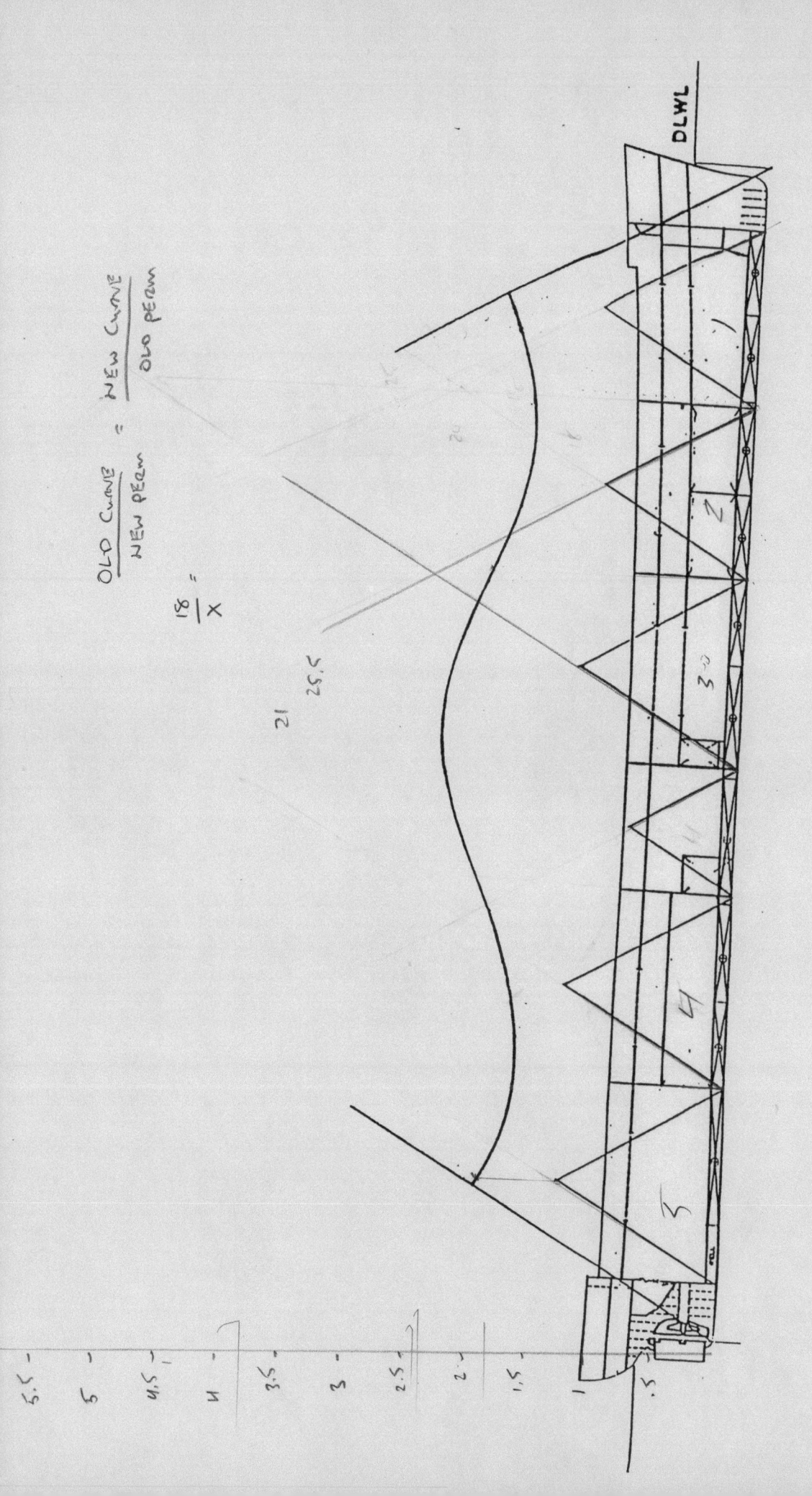

$$\frac{\text{OLD CURVE}}{\text{NEW PERM}} = \frac{\text{NEW CURVE}}{\text{OLD PERM}}$$

$$\frac{18}{x} =$$

TRIM
AND
STABILITY BOOKLET
FOR
SINGLE SCREW CARGO VESSEL

S.S. AMERICAN MARINER

C4-S-1a

OFFICIAL NO.

PREPARED BY:
DIVISION OF PRELIMINARY DESIGN
OFFICE OF SHIP CONSTRUCTION
MARITIME ADMINISTRATION
U.S. DEPARTMENT OF COMMERCE

APPROVED BY

NAME —

_____
CHIEF, DIVISION OF PRELIMINARY DESIGN   DATE

TABLE OF PRINCIPAL CHARACTERISTICS

LENGTH, OVERALL	563'-7 3/4"	PASSENGERS	12
LENGTH, B.P.	528'-0"	CREW	58
LENGTH, 20 STATIONS	520'-0"	GRAIN CUBIC	837,305 CU. FT.
BEAM, MOLDED	76'-0"	BALE CUBIC	736,723 "
DEPTH TO MAIN DK., MLD. AT SIDE	44'-6"	REEFER CUBIC	30,254 "
DEPTH TO 2ND. DK., MLD. AT SIDE	35'-6"	FUEL OIL (D.B.'S + SETTLERS)	2652 TONS
BULKHEAD DK.	2ND. DK	FUEL OIL (DEEP TANKS)	1156 "
MACHINERY	TURBINE	FUEL OIL, TOTAL	3808 "
DESIGNED SEA SPEED	20 KNOTS	FRESH WATER	257 "
SHAFT HORSEPOWER, NORMAL	17,500	NO. OF HOLDS	7
SHAFT HORSEPOWER, MAXIMUM	19,250	GROSS TONNAGE	9215
FULL LOAD DRAFT, MLD.	29'-9"	NET TONNAGE	5367
FULL LOAD DISPLACEMENT	21,093 TONS		
LIGHTSHIP	7,675 "		
LIGHTSHIP VCG	31.5'		
LIGHTSHIP LCG AFT F.P.	276.5'		

SHEET 1

C4-S-1a

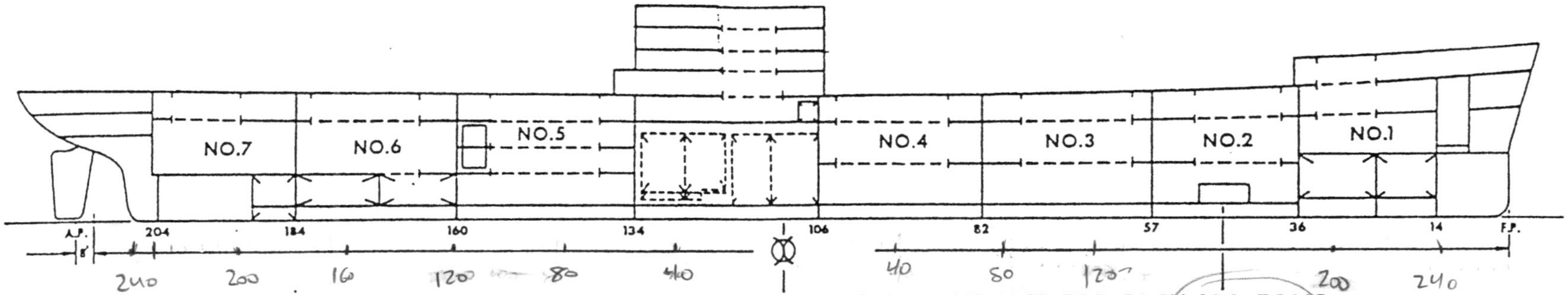

TABLE OF CORRECTIONS IN INCHES TO DRAFT FORWARD AND AFT FOR EACH 100 TONS LOADED AT ANY DISTANCE FROM AMIDSHIPS.

EXAMPLE – FIND THE CHANGE IN TRIM AFTER LOADING 100 TONS IN NO. 2 HOLD (160 FEET FORWARD AMIDSHIPS)

```
INITIAL DRAFT    FORWARD  19'-6"    AFT  20'-6"
CORRECTION       FORWARD   +7.6"    AFT   -4"
NEW DRAFT                 20'-2"        20'-2"
```

30'-0" DRAFT

| FOR'D | +7.1 | +6.8 | -5.0 | -5.3 | +9.0 | +9.0 | -5.3 | -4.8 | +8.5 | +8.5 | -4.6 | -4.3 | +8.2 | +7.9 | -4.1 | -3.8 | +7.6 | +7.4 | -3.6 | -3.4 | +7.1 | +6.8 | -3.1 | -2.9 | +6.5 | +6.2 | -2.7 | -2.4 | +6.0 | +5.7 | -2.2 | -1.9 | +5.4 | +5.1 | -1.7 | -1.5 | +4.6 | +4.3 | -1.2 | -1.0 | +4.0 | +3.7 | -0.8 | -0.5 | +3.4 | +3.2 | -0.3 | 0 | +2.9 | +2.6 | +0.2 | +0.4 | +2.3 | +2.0 | +0.7 | +0.9 | +1.8 | +1.5 | +1.1 | +1.4 | +1.2 | +0.9 | +1.6 | +1.9 | +0.6 | +0.4 | +2.1 | +2.3 | +0.1 | -0.2 | +2.6 | +2.8 | -0.5 | -0.8 | +3.0 | +3.3 | -1.1 | -1.3 | +3.5 | +3.8 | -1.6 | -1.9 | +4.0 | +4.2 | -2.2 | -2.5 | +4.5 | +4.7 | -2.7 | -3.0 | +4.9 | +5.2 | -3.3 | -3.6 | +5.4 | +5.7 | -3.9 | -4.1 | +5.9 | +6.1 | -4.4 |

20'-0" DRAFT

NOTES
1. THE CORRECTIONS HAVE BEEN COMPUTED FOR THE TWO DRAFTS 10 FEET APART TO FACILITATE INTERPOLATION, BUT IN PRACTICE IT WILL BE ACCURATE ENOUGH TO REFER TO THE TABLE NEAREST THE SHIP'S DRAFT.
2. WHEN DISCHARGING, USE THE TABLE AS LOADING AND CHANGE THE PLUS AND MINUS SIGNS.

SCALE 1" = 50'

SHEET 2

HYDROSTATIC PROPERTIES
C4-S-1a

MEAN DRAFT BOTTOM OF KEEL	TOTAL DISP. S.W. TONS	TRANSVERSE KM MLD. FEET	TONS PER INCH IMMERSION	MOMENT TO TRIM 1" FT. TONS	L.C.B. AFT E.P. FEET	L.C.F. AFT E.P. FEET	MEAN DRAFT BOTTOM OF KEEL
30		31.4		1950		282	30
	21000		70		269	281	
29		31.3		1900			29
	20000	31.2	69	1850		280	
28							28
	19000	31.1		1800	268	279	
27			68				27
				1750		278	
26	18000						26
			67	1700		277	
25		31.05			267		25
	17000			1650		276	
24		31.1	66			275	24
	16000			1600			
23		31.2			266	274	23
	15000	31.3	65	1550			
22		31.4				273	22
		31.5	64				
21	14000	31.6		1500		272	21
		31.8			265		
20	13000	32.0	63			271	20
19		32.5		1450		270	19
	12000						
18		33.0	62				18
					264	269	
17	11000	33.5		1400			17
16		34.0	61			268	16
	10000	34.5					
15		35.0				267	15
		35.5		1350			
	9000	36.0	60		263		
14		37.0				266	14
13	8000	38.0	59	1300		265	13
12							12

SHEET 3

TABLE FOR FREE SURFACE CORRECTION AND TANK CAPACITIES
C4-S-1a

TANK		FRAMES	TANK CAPACITY 97% F.O. TONS	TANK CAPACITY 100% S.W. TONS	FREE SURFACE CORRECTION COL A i SLACK	FREE SURFACE CORRECTION COL B i 97%	V.C.G.	L.C.G. F.P.
D.B.1	℄	14-24	48.2	52.8	106	67	4.5	39.9
D.B.1A	℄	24-36	81.9	89.8	464	204	4.8	64.9
D.B.2	P	36-57	71.2	78.1	428	158	2.7	106.6
	S	36-57	71.2	78.1	428	158	2.7	106.6
D.B.3	℄	57-82	227.6	249.5	3777	944	2.5	161.6
	P	57-82	55.6	61.0	300	120	3.0	169.2
	S	57-82	55.6	61.0	300	120	3.0	169.2
D.B.4	℄	82-106	224.1	245.7	3626	943	2.5	222.0
	P	82-106	128.1	140.5	1138	364	2.6	223.8
	S	82-106	128.1	140.5	1138	364	2.6	223.8
D.B.5	℄	106-127	196.2	215.1	3173	825	2.5	278.3
	P	106-134	178.0	195.2	2048	676	2.6	288.3
	S	106-134	180.0	197.4	2048	676	2.6	288.3
D.B.6	℄	134-160	242.3	265.7	3928	1021	2.5	354.4
	P	134-160	87.0	95.4	615	221	2.8	348.2
	S	134-160	87.0	95.4	615	221	2.8	348.2
D.B.7	P	160-184	94.6	103.7	768	269	2.7	412.4
	S	160-184	94.6	103.7	768	269	2.7	412.4
D.T.1	℄	14-24	125.3	137.4	134	130	16.5	40.3
D.T.1A	℄	24-36	257.6	282.5	945	680	16.8	65.1
D.T.2	P	106-113	100.7		20	20	19.1	260.8
	S	106-113	100.7		20	20	19.1	260.8
D.T.3	P	113-119	86.1		17	17	19.1	277.0
	S	113-119	86.1		17	17	19.1	277.0
D.T.6	P	160-172	201.2	220.7	1242	634	11.4	401.2
	S	160-172	201.2	220.7	1242	634	11.4	401.2
D.T.7	P	172-184	128.8	141.2	618	358	11.7	430.7
	S	172-184	128.8	141.2	618	358	11.7	430.7
D.T.8	P	184-190	50.5	55.4	68	58	9.6	454.0
	S	184-190	50.5	55.4	68	58	9.6	454.0

TANK		FRAMES	TANK CAPACITY 100% F.W TONS	TANK CAPACITY 100% S.W. TONS	F.S. CORR. COL C i SLACK	V.C.G.	L.C.G. F.P.
FORE PEAK	℄	STEM-14		110.8		11.7	17.1
AFT PEAK	℄	204-218		93.0		24.9	506.8
D.T.4	P/S	120-127	123.7		5575	21.3	296.0
D.T.5	P/S	127-133	108.4		4789	20.9	312.0
DIST. WATER	℄	106-109	24.9		59	39.5	255.8

NOTES:

FUEL OIL AT 37.23 CU.FT./TON-97% FULL
FRESH WATER AT 36.0 CU. FT./TON-100% FULL
SALT WATER AT 35.0 CU. FT./TON-100% FULL

FREE SURFACE CORRECTION PROCEDURE

ADD QUANTITY IN COLUMN A FOR TANKS SLACK
ADD QUANTITY IN COLUMN B FOR TANKS 97% FULL
ADD QUANTITY IN COLUMN C FOR F.W. TANKS
IF ANY TANK IS EMPTY, OR PRESSED UP WITH WATER, USE ZERO FOR THAT TANK.

DIVIDE SUM TOTAL BY THE SHIP DISPLACEMENT IN TONS TO OBTAIN FREE SURFACE CORRECTION IN FEET.

GAIN IN GM BY BALLASTING (FEET)
C4-S-1a

TANK	D.B.1	D.B.1A	D.B.2	D.B.3	D.B.4	D.B.5	D.B.6	D.B.7	D.T.1	D.T.1A	D.T.6	D.T.7	D.T.8
TONS	52	89	156	371	526	607	456	207	137	282	441	282	110
85	.05	.05	.20	.40	.60	.65	.55	.20	-.10	-.15	.05	0	0
90	"	"	"	.45	"	.70	"	"	-.05	-.10	.10	.05	"
95	"	.10	"	"	.65	"	"	.25	"	"	.15	"	"
100	"	"	"	"	"	.75	.60	"	0	-.05	"	.10	.05
105	"	"	"	.50	.70	"	"	"	"	0	.20	"	"
110	"	"	"	"	"	.80	"	"	"	"	.25	.15	"
115	"	"	"	"	"	"	"	"	.05	.05	-.30	"	.10
120	"	"	"	"	"	.85	"	"	"	"	"	.20	"
-125	"	"	"	"	"	"	.65	.30	"	.10	.35	"	"
130	"	"	"	"	"	"	"	"	"	"	"	"	"
135	"	"	"	"	"	"	"	"	"	"	"	"	"
140	"	"	.25	"	"	"	"	"	"	.15	"	.25	"
145	"	"	"	"	"	"	"	"	"	"	"	"	"
150	"	"	"	"	"	"	"	"	.10	"	.40	"	"
155	"	"	"	"	"	"	"	"	"	"	"	"	"
160	"	"	"	"	"	"	"	"	"	"	"	"	"
165	"	"	"	"	"	"	"	"	"	"	"	"	"
170	"	"	"	"	"	"	"	"	"	.20	"	"	"
175	"	"	"	"	"	"	"	"	"	"	"	"	"
180	.10	"	"	"	"	"	"	"	"	"	"	"	"
185	"	"	"	"	"	"	"	"	"	"	"	"	"
190	"	"	"	"	"	"	"	"	"	"	"	"	"
195	"	"	"	"	"	"	"	"	"	"	"	"	"
200	"	"	"	"	"	"	"	"	"	"	"	"	.15
205	"	"	"	"	"	"	"	"	"	"	"	.30	"
210	"	"	"	"	"	"	"	"	"	"	"	"	"
213	"	"	"	"	"	"	"	"	"	"	"	"	"
215	"	"	"	"	"	"	"	"	"	"	"	"	"

DISPLACEMENT 100 TONS

REQUIRED GM CURVE
C4-S-1a

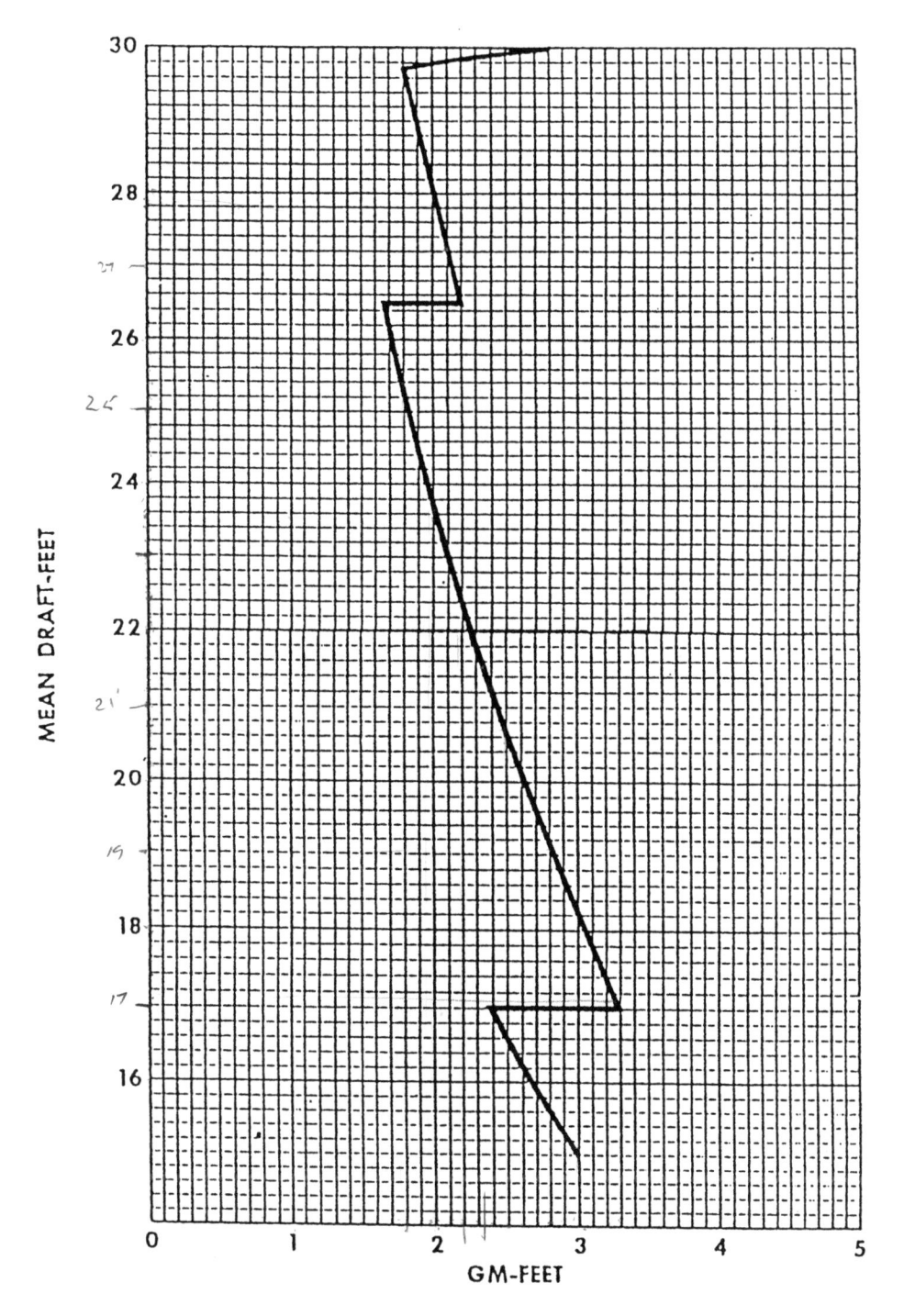

THE REQUIRED GM VALUES GIVEN IN THIS DIAGRAM MUST BE MAINTAINED IN ORDER TO ENABLE THE SHIP UNDER AVERAGE OPERATING CONDITIONS, TO SUSTAIN DAMAGE IN ANY ONE COMPARTMENT WITHOUT REACHING A CONDITION OF NEGATIVE STABILITY AFTER DAMAGE, AND WITHOUT HEELING WHICH MIGHT RESULT IN FLOODING AN UNDAMAGED COMPARTMENT.

LOADING TABLE
C4-S-1a

VOYAGE NO.

DRY CARGO

HOLD	BALE CUBIC	TONS	KG	MOMENT	LCG F.P.	MOMENT
NO.1-MAIN DK.	16085		55.6		59.2	
NO.1-2ND DK.	18140		45.2		54.8	
NO.1-3RD DK.	12210		31.9		56.6	
NO.2-2ND DK.	29255		43.0		104.4	
NO.2-3RD DK.	34592		29.1		105.3	
NO.2-TANKTOP	25476		13.1		106.2	
NO.3-2ND DK.	42000		41.3		161.3	
NO.3-3RD DK.	58150		28.3		161.6	
NO.3-TANKTOP	51375		12.7		162.7	
NO.4-2ND DK.	40255		40.3		221.5	
NO.4-3RD DK.	60020		27.7		221.9	
NO.4-TANKTOP	61140		12.5		223.1	
NO.5-2ND DK.	41775		40.5		356.5	
NO.5-26'-6" FLAT	16388		30.8		350.2	
NO.5-3RD DK.	16022		21.4		351.0	
NO.5-TANKTOP	38135		10.9		353.6	
NO.6-2ND DK.	38610		41.0		416.5	
NO.6-3RD DK.	65850		26.9		415.5	
NO.6-DEEP TANK P/S	11930		11.2		402.6	
NO.7-2ND DK.	25095		41.8		469.6	
NO.7-3RD DK.	34220		28.4		469.4	
TOTAL	736723					

REEFER CARGO

HOLD	REEFER CUBIC	TONS	KG	MOMENT	LCG F.P.	MOMENT
NO.5-26'-6" FLAT P/S	16256		30.7		354.4	
NO.5-3RD DK. P/S	13998		21.8		353.4	
TOTAL	30254					

FUEL OIL OR BALLAST

TANK	F.S.	TONS F.O-S.W.	KG	MOMENT	LCG F.P.	MOMENT
NO.1-D.B. ℄			4.5		39.9	
NO.1A-D.B. ℄			4.8		64.9	
NO.2-D.B. P/S			2.7		106.6	
NO.3-D.B. ℄			2.5		161.6	
NO.3-D.B. P/S			3.0		169.2	
NO.4-D.B. ℄			2.5		222.0	
NO.4-D.B. P/S			2.6		223.8	
NO.5-D.B. ℄			2.5		278.3	
NO.5-D.B. P/S			2.6		288.3	
NO.6-D.B. ℄			2.5		354.4	
NO.6-D.B. P/S			2.8		348.2	
NO.7-D.B. P/S			2.7		412.4	
NO.1-D.T. ℄			16.5		40.3	
NO.1A-D.T. ℄			16.8		65.1	
NO.2-D.T. P/S			19.1		260.8	
NO.3-D.T. P/S			19.1		277.0	
NO.6-D.T. P/S			11.4		401.2	
NO.7-D.T. P/S			11.7		430.7	
NO.8-D.T. P/S			9.6		454.0	
FORE PEAK			11.7		17.1	
AFTER PEAK			24.9		506.8	
TOTAL						

FRESH WATER

TANK	F.S.	TONS F.W.	KG	MOMENT	LCG F.P.	MOMENT
NO.4 D.T. P/S			21.3		296.0	
NO.5 D.T. P/S			20.9		312.0	
DIST. WATER			39.5		255.8	
TOTAL						

SHEET 7

VOYAGE NO.

ITEM	TONS	KG	MOMENT	L.C.G. F.P.	MOMENT	F.S.
LIGHTSHIP	7675	31.5	241763	276.5	2122138	✕
CREW & STORES	50	43.7	2185	276.5	13825	9
LUBE OIL	13	25.8	335	317.5	4128	
FUEL OIL & SALT WATER						
FRESH WATER						
DRY CARGO						
REEFER CARGO						
DECK CARGO						
TOTAL						

☐ DRY OR REEFER CARGO
☐ FRESH WATER
☐ FUEL OIL
☐ SALT WATER

MEAN S.W. DRAFT (SEE SHEET 3) _____
KM (SEE SHEET 3) _____
KG _____
GM _____
CORR. FOR F.S. _____
GM AVAILABLE _____
GM REQUIRED (SEE SHEET 6) _____

LCG – F.P. _____
LCB (SEE SHEET 3) _____
TRIM LEVER FWD, AFT _____
MOMENT TO TRIM 1" _____
TRIM IN INCHES FWD, AFT _____

LCF – F.P. (SHEET 3) _____
DRAFT FWD. _____
DRAFT AFT _____

SHEET 7A

DOUBLE BOTTOM TANKAGE REQUIREMENTS IN TONS TO MEET ONE COMPARTMENT DAMAGE FOR NORMAL CONDITIONS OF LOADING

TOTAL CARGO PLUS D.T. 1A, 6, 7 & 8 (COL 1+2+3)	EXCESS OF HOLD WEIGHT OVER UPPER TWEEN DECK WEIGHT IN TONS (COL 3 − COL 1)						ADDITIONAL D.B. TANKAGE PER 100 TONS OF DECK CARGO
	+1500	+1000	+500	0	−500	−1000	
1000		0	0	75	475	850	150
2000	0	0	0	800	1225	1600	140
3000	0	150	550	950	1350	1750	130
4000	0	325	675	1050	1400	1775	120
5000	50	400	750	1100	1425	1775	110
6000	100	400	725	1050	1350	1650	100
7000	50	350	650	950	1275	1600	90
8000	0	200	500	800	1100	1400	80
9000	0	0	325	650	1000	1600	70
10000	0	250	500	800	1050	1325	60
11000	0	50	325	575	825	1100	50
12000	0	0	0	275	625		

THE FOLLOWING FORMS MAY BE USED TO DETERMINE THE REQUIRED DOUBLE BOTTOM TANKAGE FROM THE ABOVE TABLE.

COL. 1			COL. 2			COL. 3	
UPPER TWEEN DK LAYER	TONS	LOWER TWEEN DK. LAYER	TONS	HOLD LAYER	TONS		
NO.1 MAIN DK.		NO.1 3RD. DK.		NO.1 DEEP TANK ℄			
" 2ND. "		" 2 "		" 1A "			
" 3 "		" 3 "		" 2 TANKTOP			
" 4 "		" 4 "		" 3 "			
" 5 "		" 5 26'-6" FLAT DRY & REEFER		" 4 "			
" 6 "		" 5 3RD. DK. "		" 5 "			
" 7 "		" 6 "		" 6 DEEP TANK P/S			
		" 7 "		" 7 "			
				" 8 "			
TOTAL	280	TOTAL	3000	TOTAL	2300		

SUMMARY

ITEM	TONS
TOTAL COL. 1	
" COL. 2	
" COL. 3	
TOTAL COL. 1+2+3	
" COL. 3 − COL. 1	
REQUIRED TANKAGE (FROM TABLE)	
DECK CARGO IN TONS = TONS	
REQUIRED D.B. TANKAGE FOR DK CARGO	
TOTAL REQUIRED D.B. TANKAGE	

SHEET 8

APPROVED
Subject to comments in
Commander, 3rd Coast Guard District (mmt)
letter of

JAN 28 1982

Chief, Merchant Marine Technical Branch
BY DIRECTION OF THE COMMANDER
AND COAST GUARD DISTRICT

S/S NORTHLAND

LOADING, TRIM & STABILITY BOOKLET

DEDICATED CLEAN BALLAST TANK CONFIGURATION

IN ACCORDANCE WITH IMCO REGULATION 13A OF 1978 PROTOCOL TO MARPOL '1973

PRODUCTS LOADING CONDITIONS

CRUDE OIL LOADING CONDITIONS

TABLE OF CONTENTS

DESCRIPTION	SHEETS
NOTES TO MASTER AND PRINCIPAL PARTICULARS	1
INSTRUCTIONS FOR COMPLETION OF TRIM AND STABILITY LOADING CONDITION FORMS	2
INSTRUCTIONS FOR COMPLETION OF FORMS TO DETERMINE HOGGING AND SAGGING NUMERALS.	3
TANK CAPACITIES AND CENTERS OF GRAVITY.	4
VERTICAL MOMENTS OF FREE SURFACE FOR LIQUIDS - FT. TONS	5
CHANGE IN DRAFTS IN INCHES FOR EACH 100 TONS ADDED.	6
CURVES OF FORM.	7
BLANK FORMS - SUMMARY, SHIP'S DEADWEIGHT, CARGO DETAILS, BALLAST DETAILS, STRENGTH.	81A-81E

NOTES TO MASTER AND PRINCIPAL PARTICULARS

1. The following cargo tanks are piped for either crude oil or clean sea water ballast (after crude oil washing):
   Cargo Tank No. 6 P,S, & CL
   Cargo Tank No. 7 P&S
   Cargo Tank No. 8 CL
   Cargo Tank No. 9 CL

2. The above-noted tanks are NOT to be used for either products cargo or sea water ballast when carrying products.

3. A light ship plus clean sea water ballast condition is included herein to demonstrate compliance with the requirements of Regulation 13A of the International Conference on Tanker Safety and Pollution Prevention, 1978.

4. The Products Loading Conditions herein are predicated on a maximum draft at bow or stern of 38.50' for transit of the Panama Canal.

5. Principal Particulars:

   Length Overall------------------------------ 736' - 3-3/4"
   Length Between Perpendiculars--------------- 705' - 0"
   Breadth Moulded----------------------------- 102' - 0"
   Depth Moulded------------------------------- 50' - 0"
   Full Load Draft Summer Freeboard------------ 39' - 9-3/4"
   Full Loaded Displacement-------------------- 62,160
   Deadweight---------------------------------- 49,339

SHEET 1

INSTRUCTIONS FOR COMPLETION OF TRIM AND STABILITY LOADING CONDITION FORMS

1. Blank forms for calculation of trim and stability for conditions not covered by this booklet are:

   Sheet 81A Summary Sheet
         81B Details of Ship's Deadweight
         81C Details of Cargo Loading
         81D Details of Sea Water Ballast

2. Enter weights and free surface on Sheets 81B, 81C and 81D as applicable. Compute moments and totals and enter on Summary Form, Sheet 81A, and compute summary totals. Take care to enter longitudinal moments as + for Aft, - for Forward.

3. For the displacement, Sheet 81A, read mean draft from Sheet 7, Curves of Form. At this draft, read Curves of Form data for KM, LCB, MT 1" and LCF. Enter these data on Sheet 81A.

4. Transverse Stability
   Subtract the total VCG (=KG) from KM to obtain the GM uncorrected for free surface. Divide the total free surface by the displacement to obtain the free surface correction and subtract this value from the uncorrected GM. The final result is the GM corrected for free surface, which must be at least 1.2 FT (to suit max req'd weather criteria GM at IMCO Ballast Draft per superseded Stability Booklet).

5. Trim
   Subtract the total LCG from the LCB to obtain the trimming lever. Trim is by stern if LCG is aft of LCB and by bow otherwise. Compute trim by multiplying displacement by trimming lever and dividing by product (MT1 x 12"). For drafts of 32 FT or greater and/or small trim, the effect of LCF on trim is small and forward and aft drafts can be computed by adding or subtracting (to suit trim by bow or stern) half the trim from the mean draft. For large trim at drafts less than 32 feet compute draft at bow = mean draft - trim X (352.5 - LCF)/705. The draft & LCF values are treated algebraically; i.e., the minus signs in the expression change to plus for trim by bow and/or LCF aft of amidships. Draft at stern is draft at bow - trim.

SHEET 2

INSTRUCTIONS FOR COMPLETION OF FORMS TO DETERMINE HOGGING AND SAGGING NUMERALS

1. Sheet 81E is the form for computing longitudinal bending stress numerals. The resulting numeral should not exceed 100.

2. The weights entered on Sheets 81B, 81C and 81D, divided by 100 and as applicable, are entered in the "Tons/100" column of Sheet 81E for departure and arrival conditions. Multiply the "Tons/100" by the Hogging and Sagging Factors for all weights entered in lines 1-27 and enter totals on line 28, "Total Deadweight."

3. Line 29 gives the light ship value for "Tons/100" and the associated hogging and sagging numerals. The light ship value includes weights for spare tailshaft and stowage as given on Sheet 81B ([12821 + 29]/100 = 128.50). Add lines 28 and 29 to obtain line 30 displacement and hogging and sagging numerals for departure and arrival conditions.

4. Enter the "Tons/100" deadweight from line 28 in line 31 "Numeral" columns for both hogging and sagging, and subtract from line 30. The resulting values in line 32 must not exceed 100.

SHEET 3

TANK CAPACITIES AND CENTERS OF GRAVITY

CARGO TANKS	FRS	BBLS 98% FULL	VCG ABV. MLD BL	LCG FROM ⊄
NO. 1 CL	102-107	15,878	26.13	227.5F
NO. 1 P/S	102-107	15,460	27.53	226.4F
NO. 2 CL	97-102	15,878	26.13	187.5F
NO. 2 P/S	97-102	18,944	26.33	187.1F
NO. 3 CL	93-97	15,878	26.13	147.5F
NO. 3 P/S	93-97	20,094	25.93	147.5F
NO. 4 CL	89-93	15,878	26.13	107.5F
NO. 4 P/S	89-93	20,254	25.93	107.5F
NO. 5 CL	85-89	15,866	26.13	67.5F
NO. 5 P/S	85-89	20,254	25.93	67.5F
NO. 6 CL	81-85	15,855	26.13	27.5F
NO. 6 P/S	81-85	20,254	25.93	27.5F
NO. 7 CL	77-81	15,367	26.13	12.5A
NO. 7 P/S	77-81	20,254	25.93	12.5A
NO. 8 CL	73-77	15,867	26.13	52.5A
NO. 8 P/S	73-77	20,254	25.93	52.5A
NO. 9 CL	69-73	15,850	26.13	92.5A
NO. 9 P/S	69-73	20,066	25.95	92.5A
NO.10 CL	65-69	15,857	26.13	132.5A
NO.10 P/S	65-69	19,364	26.23	132.3A
NO.11 CL	61-65	15,850	26.13	172.5A
NO.11 P/S	61-65	17,244	26.93	171.9A
		386,956	26.2	26.4F

FUEL OIL TANKS	FRS	CAPACITY CUBIC FT	F.O-TONS 37.23 CU.FT./LT 98% FULL	VCG ABV. MLD BL	LCG FROM ⊄
SETTLER (P)	58-60	8459	222.5	37.83	205.3A
SETTLER (S)	58-60	8441	222.5	37.83	205.3A
DEEP TANK (P)	58-60	17436	459.0	29.83	203.8A
DEEP TANK (S)	58-60	17436	459.0	29.83	203.8A
DEEP TANK (P)	108-120	52426	1354.0	29.53	267.6F
DEEP TANK (S)	108-120	57757	1513.0	28.13	265.1F
		161655	4230.0	29.7	114.6F

FRESH WATER TANKS	FRS	CAPACITY CUBIC FT	TONS 100% FULL	VCG ABV. MLD BL	LCG FROM ⊄
POTABLE (P)	13-17	1569.5	43.60	48.53	322.4A
POTABLE (S)	13-17	1118.9	31.08	48.51	321.5A
POTABLE CL	88-90	1099.0	30.25	57.43	90.0F
DISTILLED (P)	39-45	2160.0	60.00	42.73	258.5A
		5937.4	164.93		

BALLAST TANKS

	FRS	CAPACITY CUBIC FT	TONS 100% FULL	VCG ABV. MLD BL	LCG FROM ⊄
FORE PEAK	Stem-130	26198	748.5	22.03	323.0F
AFT PEAK	Stem-17	13801	394.3	36.53	333.8A
DEEP TANK (P)	120-130	30623	874.9	29.13	295.1F
DEEP TANK (S)	120-130	30521	872.0	29.13	295.1F

COFFERDAMS

	FRS	CAPACITY CUBIC FT	TONS 100% FULL	VCG ABV. MLD BL	LCG FROM ⊄
FWD (P)	107-108	4703	134.4	27.93	249.0F
FWD (S)	107-108	7134	203.8	27.93	249.0F
AFT (P)	60-61	4190	119.7	31.13	194.0A
AFT (S)	60-61	4190	119.7	31.13	194.0A

NOTES: VCG's of slack cargo & deep tanks are obtained by multiplying the VCG's shown by % fullness of tank.

SHEET 4

VERTICAL MOMENTS OF FREE SURFACE OF LIQUIDS - FT TONS

CARGO TANKS

NO.	I(FT⁴)	61° API (48.93) (CF/T) I/δ	40° API (43.58) (CF/T) I/δ	30° API (41.04) (CF/T) I/δ	14° API (36.97) (CF/T) I/δ	S.W. (35.00) (CF/T) I/δ
1 CL	283,940	5804	6515	6920	7682	8114
1 (P) OR (S)	52,000	1060	1190	1264	1403	1482
2 CL	283,940	5804	6517	6920	7682	8114
2 (P) OR (S)	77,000	1588	1783	1893	2102	2220
3 CL	283,940	5804	6517	6920	7682	8114
3 (P) OR (S)	81,100	1658	1862	1977	2195	2318
4 CL	283,940	5804	6517	6920	7682	8114
4 (P) OR (S)	81,290	1662	1866	1982	2200	2323
5 CL	283,940	5804	6517	6920	7682	8114
5 (P) OR (S)	81,290	1662	1866	1982	2200	2323
6 CL	283,940	5804	6517	6920	7682	8114
6 (P) OR (S)	81,290	1662	1866	1982	2200	2323
7 CL	283,940	5804	6517	6920	7682	8114
7 (P) OR (S)	81,290	1662	1866	1982	2200	2323
8 CL	283,940	5804	6517	6920	7682	8114
8 (P) OR (S)	81,290	1662	1866	1982	2200	2323
9 CL	283,940	5804	6517	6920	7682	8114
9 (P) OR (S)	81,290	1662	1866	1982	2200	2323
10 CL	283,940	5804	6517	6920	7682	8114
10(P) OR (S)	81,100	1658	1862	1977	2195	2318
11 CL	283,940	5804	6517	6920	7682	8114
11(P) OR (S)	77,930	1593	1789	1900	2109	2227

FUEL, FRESH WATER, BALLAST & WASH WATER

FUEL OIL	I(FT⁴)	I/δ
SETTLER (P) OR (S) FR. 58-60	11,450	308
AFT BUNKER (P) OR (S) FR. " "	30,500	819
FWD BUNKER (P) FR.108-120	160,051	4299
FWD BUNKER (S) FR. " "	160,051	4299

FRESH WATER		
STEERING RM (P) FR. 13-17	15,768	438
STEERING RM (S) FR. " "	10,728	298
DISTILLED (P) FR. 37-45	9,324	259
UNDER BRIDGE FR. BB½-90½	2,160	60

S.W. BALLAST		
FORE PEAK Stem FR. - 130	109,060	3,116
AFT PEAK FR. 17 - Stern	160,335	4,581
BALLAST (P)OR(S) FR.120-130	55,510	1,586

1. To obtain the free surface correction to GM in any condition of loading, add the I/δ values of all slack tanks and divide by the displacement of vessel.

2. Values of I/δ for different API cargo may be obtained by either dividing tabular values of I(FT⁴) by corresponding density of cargo in tank, or by interpolation.

SHEET 5

37'-0" DRAFT

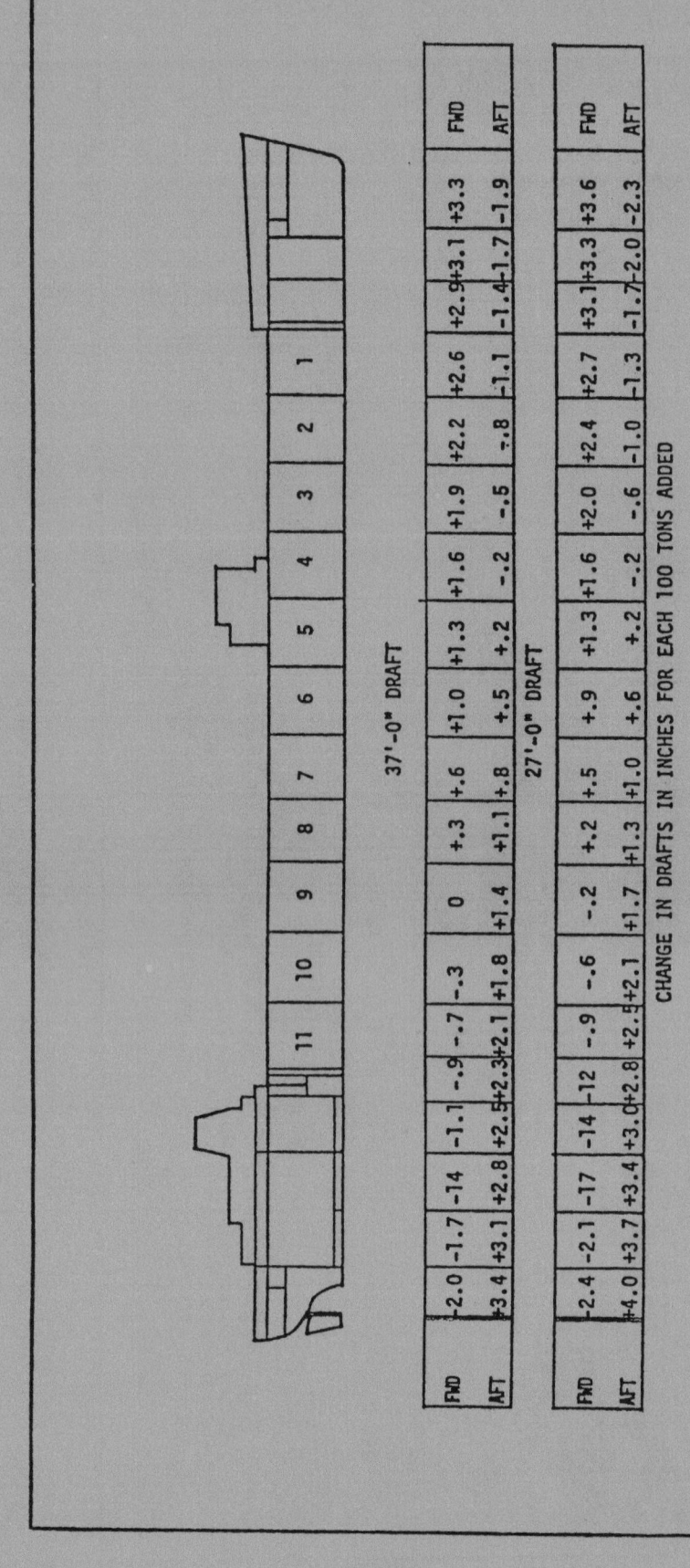

	11	10	9	8	7	6	5	4	3	2	1	
FWD	-2.0	-1.7	-1.4	-.9	-.7	-.3	0	+.3	+.6	+1.0	+1.3	+1.6	+1.9	+2.2	+2.6	+2.9	+3.1	+3.3	FWD
AFT	+3.4	+3.1	+2.8	+2.5	+2.3	+2.1	+1.8	+1.4	+1.1	+.8	+.5	+.2	-.2	-.5	-.8	-1.1	-1.4	-1.7	-1.9	AFT

27'-0" DRAFT

FWD	-2.4	-2.1	-1.7	-1.4	-1.2	-.9	-.6	-.2	+.2	+.5	+.9	+1.3	+1.6	+2.0	+2.4	+2.7	+3.1	+3.3	+3.6	FWD
AFT	+4.0	+3.7	+3.4	+3.0	+2.8	+2.5	+2.1	+1.7	+1.3	+1.0	+.6	+.2	-.2	-.6	-1.0	-1.3	-1.7	-2.0	-2.3	AFT

CHANGE IN DRAFTS IN INCHES FOR EACH 100 TONS ADDED

EXAMPLE: Add 500 Tons in No. 11 Tank

```
Original Drafts       FWD 34'-6"           AFT 33'-6"
Correction          5(-0.7)= -3½"        5(+2.1)= +10½"
New Drafts            FWD 34'-2½"          AFT 34'-4½"
```

NOTE

1. For discharging, reverse + and – signs in the table
2. Corrections for intermediate drafts may be interpreted from the table.

SHEET 6

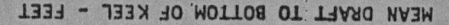

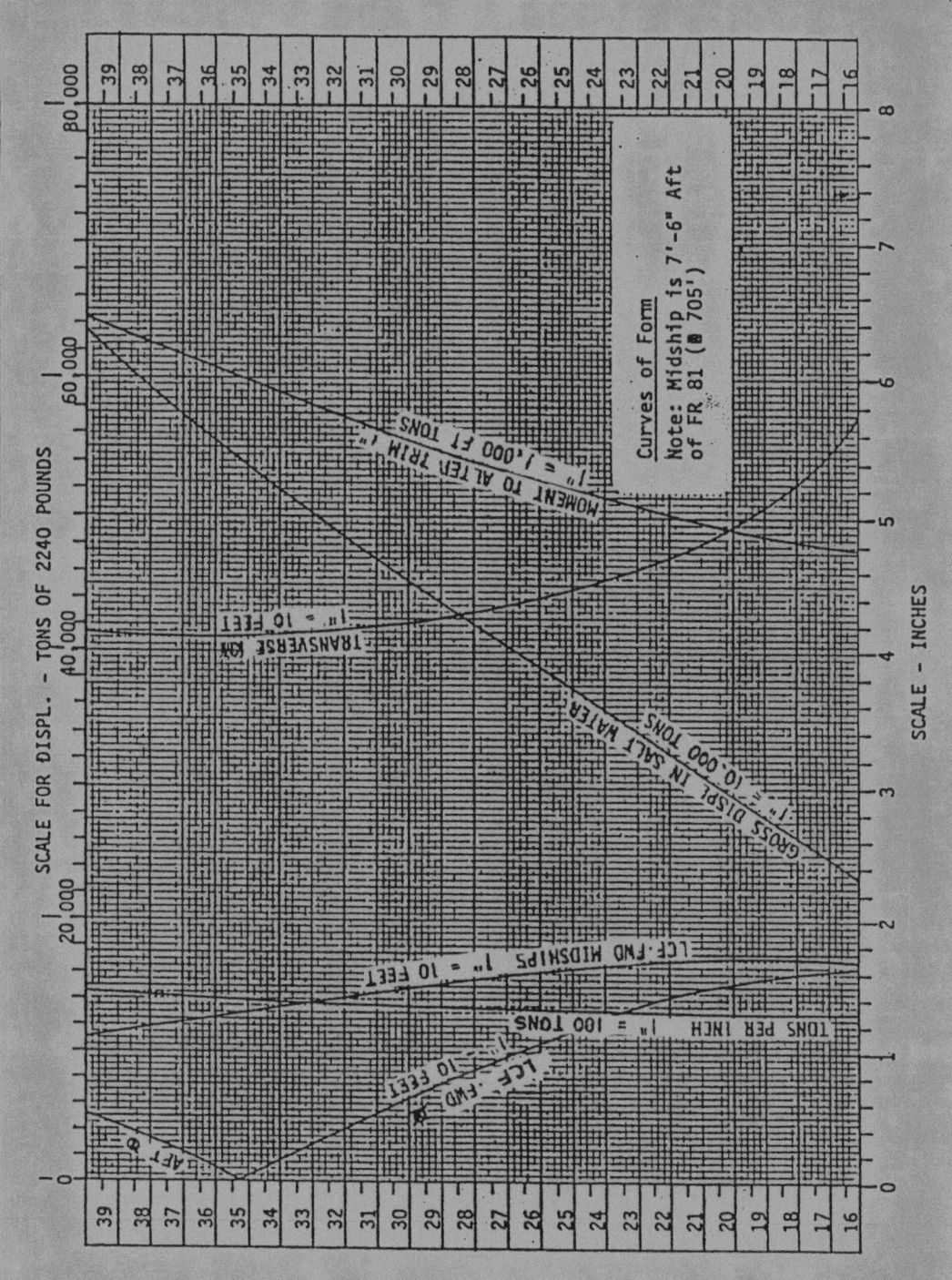

SHEET 7

LOADING SUMMARY

CONDITION:

LEGEND
- CARGO
- BALLAST WATER
- FRESH WATER
- FUEL OIL

DESCRIPTION	L. TONS	VCG ABOVE BL (FT)	VERTICAL MOMENT (FT TONS)	LCG FROM ⊥ FT (+ = AFT)	LONGITUDINAL MOMENT (FT TONS)	FREE SURFACE (FT TONS)
LIGHT SHIP	12821	32.23	413,221	23.06 A	295,652	
SHIP'S DEADWEIGHT - SHEET 81B						
CARGO - SHEET 81C						
CLEAN S.W. BALLAST - SHEET 81D						
TOTALS						

STABILITY

MEAN DRAFT AT LCF .... FT
KM .... FT
KG .... FT
GM (uncorr) .... FT
F.S. correction .... FT
GM AVAILABLE .... FT

TRIM

LCF ....
LCB ....
LCG ....
TRIM LVR ...
MT 1" ......
TRIM .... FT TONS
DRAFT - FP =
DRAFT - AP =

SHEET 81A

DETAILS OF SHIP'S DEADWEIGHT - CONDITION _____

DESCRIPTION	L. TONS	VCG ABOVE BL (FT)	VERTICAL MOMENT (FT TONS)	LCG FROM ℄ FT (+ = AFT)	LONGITUDINAL MOMENT (FT TONS)	FREE SURFACE (FT TONS)
CREW & EFFECTS - DECK HOUSE	3	68.23	205	90.0 F	- 270	-
CREW & EFFECTS - AFT HOUSE	7	56.23	394	256.0 A	1792	-
SPARE TAIL SHAFT & STOWAGE	29	8.23	239	298.5 A	8656	-
TOTAL CONSTANTS	(39)	21.5	(838)	261.0 A	(10178)	-
STORES - FORWARD		54.23		307.0 F		-
- DECK HOUSE		54.23		90.0 F		-
- AFT HOUSE		54.23		276.3 A		-
FRESH WATER - UNDER BRIDGE		57.43		90.0 F		
- DISTILLED		42.73		258.5 A		
- STEERG GR RM (P)		48.53		322.4A		
- STEERG GR RM (S)		48.53		321.5A		
FUEL OIL - AFT BUNKER (P)		29.83		203.8A		
- AFT BUNKER (S)		29.83		203.8A		
- SETTLER (P)		37.83		205.3A		
- SETTLER (S)		37.83		205.3A		
- FWD BUNKER (P)		29.53		267.6F		
- FWD BUNKER. (S)		28.13		265.1F		
TOTALS						

CARGO –

DESCRIPTION	L. TONS	VCG ABOVE BL (FT)	VERTICAL MOMENT (FT TONS)	LCG FROM ℄ FT (+ = AFT)	LONGITUDINAL MOMENT (FT TONS)	FREE SURFACE (FT TONS)
NO. 1 CL		26.13		227.5 F		
NO. 1 P/S		27.53		226.4 F		
NO. 2 CL		26.13		187.5 F		
NO. 2 P/S		26.33		187.1 F		
NO. 3 CL		26.13		147.5 F		
NO. 3 P/S		25.93		147.5 F		
NO. 4 CL		26.13		107.5 F		
NO. 4 P/S		25.93		107.5 F		
NO. 5 CL		26.13		67.5 F		
NO. 5 P/S		25.93		67.5 F		
NO. 6 CL		26.13		27.5 F		
NO. 6 P/S		25.93		27.5 F		
NO. 7 CL		26.13		12.5 A		
NO. 7 P/S		25.93		12.5 A		
NO. 8 CL		26.13		52.5 A		
NO. 8 P/S		25.93		52.5 A		
NO. 9 CL		26.13		92.5 A		
NO. 9 P/S		25.93		92.5 A		
NO. 10 CL		26.13		132.5 A		
NO. 10 P/S		26.23		132.3 A		
NO. 11 CL		26.13		172.5 A		
NO. 11 P/S		26.93		172.9 A		
TOTALS						

CONDITION:

DETAILS OF CLEAN SEA WATER BALLAST

DESCRIPTION	L. TONS	VCG ABOVE BL (FT)	VERTICAL MOMENT (FT TONS)	LCG FROM ₵ FT (+ = AFT)	LONGITUDINAL MOMENT (FT TONS)	FREE SURFACE (FT TONS)
ORIGINAL CLEAN BALLAST TANKS:						
FORE PEAK		22.03		323.0 F		
AFT PEAK		36.53		333.8 A		
DEEP TANK, P/S		29.13		295.1 F		
NO. 6 SIDE TANK P/S		25.93		27.5 F		
TANKS CONVERTED TO CLEAN BALLAST:						
NO. 6 TANK, CL		26.13		27.5 F		
NO. 7 SIDE TANK, P/S		25.93		12.5 A		
NO. 8 TANK, CL		26.13		52.5 A		
NO. 9 TANK, CL		26.13		92.5 A		
FORWARD COFFERDAM		27.93		249.0 F		
AFT COFFERDAM		31.13		194.0 A		
TOTALS						

SHEET 81D

LONGITUDINAL BENDING STRESSES (PSI)

CONDITION:

		DEPARTURE				ARRIVAL			
			HOGGING		SAGGING			HOGGING		SAGGING
DESCRIPTION	TONS/100	FACTOR	NUMERAL	FACTOR	NUMERAL	TONS/100	FACTOR	NUMERAL	FACTOR	NUMERAL
1. FORE PEAK		1.64		0.30			1.64		0.30	
2. DEEP TANK P/S		1.53		0.42			1.53		0.42	
3. FWD STORES		1.51		0.44			1.51		0.44	
4. FWD BUNKERS		1.43		0.54			1.43		0.54	
5. FWD COFFERDAM		1.36		0.61			1.36		0.61	
6. #1 CARGO TANK		1.28		0.70			1.28		0.70	
7. #2 CARGO TANK		1.14		0.86			1.14		0.86	
8. #3 CARGO TANK		1.00		1.02			1.00		1.02	
9. #4 CARGO TANK		0.85		1.18			0.85		1.18	
10. BRIDGE CREW		0.78		1.25			0.78		1.25	
11. BRIDGE STORES		0.78		1.25			0.78		1.25	
12. BRIDGE F.W.		0.78		1.25			0.78		1.25	
13. #5 CARGO TANK		0.70		1.35			0.70		1.35	
14. #6 BALLAST TANK		0.56		1.51			0.56		1.51	
15. #7 CARGO/BALLAST TANK		0.51		1.57			0.51		1.57	
16. #8 CARGO/BALLAST TANK		0.67		1.43			0.67		1.43	
17. #9 CARGO/BALLAST TANK		0.83		1.28			0.83		1.28	
18. #10 CARGO TANK		1.00		1.14			1.00		1.14	
19. #11 CARGO TANK		1.16		0.99			1.16		0.99	
20. AFT COFFERDAM		1.26		0.90			1.26		0.90	
21. AFT BUNKERS		1.28		0.88			1.28		0.88	
22. AFT SETTLERS		1.29		0.87			1.29		0.87	
23. DISTILLED WATER		1.51		0.67			1.51		0.67	
24. AFT STORES		1.56		0.61			1.56		0.61	
25. AFT CREW		1.50		0.68			1.50		0.68	
26. F.W. AFT		1.77		0.44			1.77		0.44	
27. AFT PEAK		1.82		0.40			1.82		0.40	
28. TOTAL DEADWEIGHT	128.50		83.63		14.01	128.50		83.63		14.01
29. LIGHT SHIP										
30. DISPLACEMENT										
31. DEADWEIGHT CORRECTION -LINE 28 WEIGHT										
32. NUMERAL (MAY NOT EXCEED 100)										

SHEET 81E